VOLUME SEVEN

Greetings from Heaven

Direction for Our Times
As given to Anne,
a lay apostle

VOLUME SEVEN

Direction for Our Times
As given to Anne, a lay apostle

ISBN: 978-0-9766841-6-9

Library of Congress Number: applied for

Publisher: Direction for Our Times

In Ireland:	In the USA:
Direction for Our Times	Direction for Our Times
The Hague Building	9000 West 81st Street
Cullies	Justice, IL 60458
Cavan	USA
Co. Cavan	
Ireland	
+353-(0)49-437-3040	708-496-9300

www.directionforourtimes.org

How to Pray the Rosary information, is used with permission. Copyright © Congregation of Marians of the Immaculate Conception, Stockbridge, MA 01263. www.marian.org.

Paintings of *Jesus Christ the Returning King* and *Our Lady Queen of the Church* by Janusz Antosz

V0515

Nihil Obstat: Very Rev. John Canon Murphy, PP, VF

Imprimatur: ✠ Most Rev. Leo O'Reilly,
              Bishop of Kilmore, Ireland.

DIOCESE OF KILMORE

Tel: 049 4331496
Fax: 049 4361796
Email: bishop@kilmorediocese.ie
Website: www.kilmorediocese.ie

Bishop's House
Cullies
Cavan
Co. Cavan

To Whom It May Concern:

Direction For Our Times (DFOT) is a religious movement founded by "Anne", a lay apostle from our diocese, who wishes to remain anonymous. The movement is in its infancy and does not as yet enjoy canonical status. I have asked a priest of the diocese, Fr.Connolly, to assist in the work of the movement and to ensure that in all its works and publications it remains firmly within the teaching and practice of the Catholic Church.

I have known "Anne", the founder of the movement, for several years. She is a Catholic in good standing in the diocese, a wife and mother of small children, and a woman of deep spirituality. From the beginning she has always been anxious that everything connected with the movement be subject to the authority of the Church. She has submitted all her writings to me and will not publish anything without my permission. She has submitted her writings to the Congregation of the Doctrine of the Faith and I have done so as well.

In so far as I am able to judge she is orthodox in her writings and teachings. Her spirituality and the spiritual path that she proposes to those who wish to accept it are in conformity with the teachings of the Church and of the great spiritual writers of the past and present.

Leo O'Reilly.

Date 16 June '06

+Leo O'Reilly
Bishop of Kilmore

Diocesan Seal

DIOCESE OF KILMORE

Tel: 049-4331496
Fax: 049-4361796
Email: bishop@kilmorediocese.ie
Website: www.kilmorediocese.ie

Bishop's House
Cullies
Cavan
Co. Cavan

2 September 2011

To Whom It May Concern:

I offer an update on the present status of Anne, a lay apostle and Direction for Our Times.

I initially granted permission for the distribution of the messages and written materials of Anne. This position remains unchanged. The writings and materials may continue to be distributed. As pointed out in my letter on the DFOT website, the permission to distribute the messages does not imply a final judgment on whether they are authentic private revelation. A final judgment on that question must await the outcome of an official Church inquiry into these matters.

Following Church protocol, I set up a diocesan commission over a year ago to inquire into the writings of Anne and to evaluate her reports of receiving messages from heaven. That work of evaluation is continuing and the outcome of it will be made public in due course.

I hope this statement is helpful in the clarification of these matters.

Yours sincerely in Christ,

Leo O'Reilly
Bishop of Kilmore.

October 11, 2004

Dear Friends,

I am very much impressed with the messages delivered by Anne who states that they are received from God the Father, Jesus, and the Blessed Mother. They provide material for excellent and substantial meditation for those to whom they are intended, namely to the laity, to bishops and priests; and sinners with particular difficulties. These messages should not be read hurriedly but reserved for a time when heartfelt recollection and examination can be made.

I am impressed by the complete dedication of Anne to the authority of the magisterium, to her local Bishop and especially to the Holy Father. She is a very loyal daughter of the Church.

Sincerely in Christ,

Philip M. Hannan

Archbishop Philip M. Hannan, (Ret.)
President of FOCUS Worldwide Network
Retired Archbishop of New Orleans

PMH/aac

Dr. Mark I. Miravalle, S.T.D.

Professor of Theology and Mariology, Franciscan University of Steubenville
313 High Street • Hopedale, OH 43976 • U.S.A.
740-937-2277 • mmiravalle@franciscan.edu

Without in any way seeking to anticipate the final and definitive judgment of the local bishop and of the Holy See (to which we owe our filial obedience of mind and heart), I wish to manifest my personal discernment concerning the nature of the messages received by "Anne," a Lay Apostle.

After an examination of the reported messages and an interview with the visionary herself, I personally believe that the messages received by "Anne" are of supernatural origin.

The message contents are in conformity with the faith and morals teachings of the Catholic Church's Magisterium and in no way violate orthodox Catholic doctrine. The phenomena of the precise manner of how the messages are transmitted (i.e., the locutions and visions) are consistent with the Church's historical precedence for authentic private revelation. The spiritual fruits (cf. Mt. 7:17-20) of Christian faith, conversion, love, and interior peace, based particularly upon a renewed awareness of the indwelling Christ and prayer before the Blessed Sacrament, have been significantly manifested in various parts of the world within a relatively brief time since the messages have been received and promulgated. Hence the principal criteria used by ecclesiastical commissions to investigate reported supernatural events (message, phenomena, and spiritual fruits) are, in my opinion, substantially satisfied in the case of "Anne's" experience.

The messages which speak of the coming of Jesus Christ, the "Returning King" do not refer to an imminent end of the world with Christ's final physical coming, but rather call for a spiritual receptivity to an ongoing spiritual return of Jesus Christ, a dynamic advent of Jesus which ushers in a time of extraordinary grace and peace for humanity (in ways similar to the Fatima promise for an eventual era of peace as a result of the Triumph of the Immaculate Heart of Mary, or perhaps the "new springtime" for the Church referred to by the words of the great John Paul II).

As "Anne" has received permission from her local ordinary, Bishop Leo O'Reilly, for the spreading of her messages, and has also submitted all her writings to the Congregation for the Doctrine of the Faith, I would personally encourage, (as the Church herself permits), the prayerful reading of these messages, as they have constituted an authentic spiritual benefit for a significant number of Catholic leaders throughout the world.

Mark Miravalle

Dr. Mark Miravalle
Professor of Theology and Mariology
Franciscan University of Steubenville
October 13, 2006

Table of Contents

Introduction

Dear Reader,

I am a wife, mother of six, and a Secular Franciscan.

At the age of twenty, I was divorced for serious reasons and with pastoral support in this decision. In my mid-twenties I was a single parent, working and bringing up a daughter. As a daily Mass communicant, I saw my faith as sustaining and had begun a journey toward unity with Jesus, through the Secular Franciscan Order or Third Order.

My sister travelled to Medjugorje and came home on fire with the Holy Spirit. After hearing of her beautiful pilgrimage, I experienced an even more profound conversion. During the following year I experienced various levels of deepened prayer, including a dream of the Blessed Mother, where she asked me if I would work for Christ. During the dream she showed me that this special spiritual work would mean I would be separated from others in the world. She actually showed me my extended family and how I would be separated from them. I told her that I did not care. I would do anything asked of me.

Shortly after, I became sick with endometriosis. I have been sick ever since, with one thing or another. My sicknesses are always the types that mystify doctors in the beginning. This is part of the cross and I mention it because so many suffer in this way. I was told by my doctor that I would never conceive children. As a single parent, this did not concern me as I assumed it was God's will. Soon after, I met a wonderful man. My first marriage had been annulled and we married and conceived five children.

Spiritually speaking, I had many experiences that included what I now know to be interior locutions. These moments were beautiful and the words still stand out firmly in my heart, but I did not get excited because I was busy offering up illnesses and exhaustion. I took it as a matter of course that Jesus had to work hard to sustain me as He had given me a lot to handle. In looking back, I see that He was preparing me to do His work. My preparation period was long, difficult and not very exciting. From the outside, I think people thought, 'That woman has bad luck.' From the inside, I saw that while my sufferings were painful and long lasting, my little family was growing in love, in size and in wisdom, in the sense that my husband and I certainly understood what was important and what was not important. Our continued crosses did that for us.

Various circumstances compelled my husband and me to move with our children far from my loved ones. I offered this up and must say it is the most difficult thing I have had to contend with. Living in exile brings many beautiful opportunities to align with Christ's will; however, you have to continually remind yourself that you are doing that. Otherwise you just feel sad. After several years in exile, I finally got the inspiration to go to Medjugorje. It was actually a gift from my husband for my fortieth birthday. I had tried to go once before, but circumstances prevented the trip and I understood it was not God's will. Finally, though, it was time and my eldest daughter and I found ourselves in front of St. James Church. It was her second trip to Medjugorje.

I did not expect or consider that I would experience anything out of the ordinary. At any rate, we had a beautiful five days. I experienced a spiritual healing on the mountain. My daughter rested and prayed. A quiet but significant thing happened to me. During my Communions, I spoke with Jesus conversationally. I thought this was beautiful, but it had happened before on occasion so I was not stunned or overcome. I remember telling others that Communions in Medjugorje were powerful. I came home, deeply grateful to Our Lady for bringing us there.

The conversations continued all that winter. At some time in the six months that followed our trip, the conversations leaked into my life and came at odd times throughout the day. Jesus began to direct me with decision and I found it more and more difficult to refuse when He asked me to do this or that. I told no one.

During this time, I also began to experience direction from the Blessed Mother. Their voices are not hard to distinguish. I do not hear them in an auditory way, but in my soul or mind. By this time I knew that something remarkable was occurring and Jesus was telling me that He had special work for me, over and above my primary vocation as wife and mother. He told me to write the messages down and that He would arrange to have them published and disseminated. Looking back, it took Him a long time to get me comfortable enough where I was willing to trust Him. I trust His voice now and will continue to do my best to serve Him, given my constant struggle with weaknesses, faults, and the pull of the world.

Please pray for me as I continue to try to serve Jesus. Please answer "yes" to Him because He so badly needs us and He is so kind. He will take you right into His heart if you let Him. I am praying for you and am so grateful to God that He has given you these words. Anyone who knows Him must fall in love with Him, such is His goodness. If you have been struggling, this is your answer. He is coming to you in a special way through these words and the graces that flow through them.

Please do not fall into the trap of thinking that He cannot possibly mean for you to reach high levels of holiness. As I say somewhere in my writings, the greatest sign of the times is Jesus having to make do with the likes of me as His secretary. I consider myself the B-team, dear friends. Join me and together we will do our little bit for Him.

Message received from Jesus immediately following my writing of the above biographical information:

You see, My child, that you and I have been together for a long time. I was working quietly in your life for years before you began this work. Anne, how I love you. You can look back through your life and see so many "yes" answers to Me. Does that not please you and make you glad? You began to say "yes" to Me long before you experienced extraordinary graces. If you had not, My dearest, I could never have given you the graces or assigned this mission to you. Do you see how important it was that you got up every day, in your ordinary life, and said "yes" to your God, despite difficulty, temptation, and hardship? You could not see the big plan as I saw it. You had to rely on your faith. Anne, I tell you today, it is still that way. You cannot see My plan, which is bigger than your human mind can accept. Please continue to rely on your faith as it brings Me such glory. Look at how much I have been able to do with you, simply because you made a quiet and humble decision for Me. Make another quiet and humble decision on this day and every day, saying, "I will serve God." Last night you served Me by bringing comfort to a soul in pain. You decided against yourself and for Me, through your service to him. There was gladness in heaven, Anne. You are Mine. I am yours. Stay with Me, My child. Stay with Me.

The Allegiance Prayer
For All Lay Apostles

Dear God in Heaven, I pledge my allegiance to You. I give You my life, my work and my heart. In turn, give me the grace of obeying Your every direction to the fullest possible extent. Amen.

Part One:
Saints—Week One

July 5, 2004
St. Therese, the Little Flower

Jesus, in His merciful goodness, has willed that many saints in Heaven will come to the assistance of souls on earth. Dear holy souls, you are approaching difficult days. You know this, of course, if the Spirit is active within you. Your world is in darkness and must be cleansed. All of this has been said. What our Lord wills at this time is that we, your heavenly brothers and sisters, provide you with specific information and guidelines. Pray for discernment and you will see that there is no other path than the path that leads to Heaven and to Jesus Christ.

The time of darkness nears. The world has not converted, despite the efforts of many, both in Heaven and on earth. Souls cling rebelliously to sinful ways and do not even fear God's justice. They have embraced evil. Brothers and sisters, this world is no longer an appropriate place for God's children. It is neither safe nor conducive to the school of holiness that each soul must attend to graduate to Heaven. Little souls cannot do this here in your world because they are surrounded, literally, by the opposite of holiness. I do not wish to tell you about the sins of humanity because there was sin in my day also. I understand that sin exists and that there will always be those who choose the enemy. What I am trying to convey to you is that your world has begun to co-exist with sin in such a way that few object anymore. You are asleep, children of the world! Where are God's warriors? Too few have taken up God's cause in the past, but many will now in these times. Praise God with me, souls of earth, even as He prepares to renew your world.

In the days of confusion to come, rumors will swirl. Holy souls will be tempted to doubt authentic sites of apparition where graces flow without pause. Children, you must remain true to your calls. Jesus has placed you carefully. Serve Him. You will find yourself struggling with temptations against your missions. You will find yourself mocked. The world is going to go even further in the direction of anti-God and you will stand out even more starkly against the Godless landscape. This will not be comfortable for you but you will have complete heavenly assistance and support. Brothers and sisters, I, Therese, am only one of countless saints who has been commissioned to assist you. You will find us always near and always willing to instruct and console. We will petition the Spirit and obtain the most sublime gifts of wisdom and discernment for you. My dear fellow servants, we are entering the storm, but not without Jesus, our rudder. Children of God should not fear God's intervention. Given my heavenly knowledge, I assure you that the only fearful thing for this world would be a decision by God to leave it to itself. Welcome, brothers and sisters, to the legion of heavenly soldiers who fight for Christ. You will earn your place in Heaven.

July 6, 2004
St. Therese, the Little Flower

Brothers and sisters in the world, I bring you news from Heaven. These graces have been obtained through the years for this time. You must thank souls who have gone before you whose prayers are being used now. Truly, there is a great storehouse of graces for these days so be certain to always petition Heaven, particularly for conversions. Our goal is simple. We want to bring as many souls as possible to Heaven. In order to do that, we must bring as many people as possible to Jesus here on earth. We need conversions. We need souls to turn away from sin and follow the Gospel. There is nothing new, you are thinking. You are correct. What is new is the compelling nature of the time in which we are working. We have spoken about changes. We have spoken about a final increase in Godlessness. Now we must speak about the actual transition and how you will conduct yourselves. Be at peace in everything. That is always your first rule. You are a follower of Jesus Christ and as such your eternity is secure. There is nothing that should disturb your peace. It is very important that souls who live for the world, who are comfortable with darkness, see your peaceful, trusting countenance. Anything less will not draw them to Christ, but confirm that there is no reason to follow Christ. Next, you must be

7

concerned with your duties in life. Are you a priest? Religious? Father? Mother? Obedient son or daughter? You must live for your duty. Do your work cheerfully and honestly. In all of these things you must love. Brothers and sisters, Christ's love must shine from your eyes. Now, you do not have Christ's love unless He puts it there for you. He cannot put it there for you unless you give Him the time in silence and prayer. So our next task is really two-fold. You must always love like Christ and in order to do that you must have scheduled prayer time that includes time in silence. You know that when you spend time in Adoration and contemplation of the living Christ, you walk in calm, trusting peace. You find it easier to complete mundane tasks and love flows easily from you because He has had ample opportunity to fill your soul with divine love. I am giving you specific instructions because in order to be calm during times of upheaval, you must have sound practices and discipline. If you live simply, observing simple habits, you will have less difficulty. The world can go its way but my brothers and sisters will simply continue to follow Heaven in the beautiful fashion that Therese is outlining. You see, little brothers and sisters, I have a special role in these days. I am to assist you in walking through this time. You can rely on me. Many souls will ask for my help and they will not be disappointed. Heaven gives me great glory because I was so small on earth. You will follow my way, my dear friends, and nothing will cause you alarm because you will understand that all of Heaven watches and all of Heaven assists you.

•

St. Philomena

Souls must understand that Heaven and earth are joined. There is no separation except in the ability of earthly souls to experience Heaven. Brothers and sisters, fellow soldiers for Christ, we are with you. Jesus is with you. There are countless angels with you. Truly, Heaven is with you. Ask for more faith and more faith shall be yours. In order to have confidence, and you need confidence, you must understand what we are saying to you. View every day, every event, and every experience as something that you are seeing side by side with us. We are by your side in everything. Why is this so important? We want your view to be similar to our view. Souls discard holiness often because they think they will have to give up too much to be great saints. Do not try to be a great saint. Try to be a little saint because then you will be great, like Therese. Simply rise in the morning and do your duty, keeping Jesus as your goal. If you try to serve quietly in everything, you will become a saint in spite of yourself. If something big arises and you are in the habit of serving, you will serve easily, with very little thought. This is where practice and discipline are important. Brothers and sisters, you are to experience a time of change, but you have been prepared if you are following Jesus. If you are not, then you should begin and Jesus will prepare you. Believe me, Philomena, when I tell you that your souls will be protected. Do not fear bodily hardships because these things are fleeting. Be in the habit of denying your body a little every day. Again, this is practice. When you deny yourself, perhaps in fasting, you have not said, "I will never eat again." You have said, "I will not eat for now. I will eat later." It is the same. If you are in a position where your body is being denied something, simply tell yourself that you are being denied at the moment but not forever. You will pray and give thanks to God whatever the circumstances and souls will be saved in great numbers from your prayers of acceptance. There will be the greatest graces available so I do not fear for you because when you experience these times you will have exactly the graces you require. Jesus is so good and He loves us so much! Concentrate on this, my dear friends, and you will not nourish useless fears. We come to provide you with heavenly advice because we have walked your hardships. If you walk with Jesus Christ you have all the power you need, believe me. He will protect you and we, His saints, have the greatest sympathy and love for you. We are truly a family working together. We are working together to rescue souls from the darkness so that they will spend eternity praising our sweet Jesus.

July 8, 2004
St. Philomena

Dear brothers and sisters, you must be joyful during this time. Whenever you are tempted toward despair, you must think of Heaven and how Jesus is making the earth like Heaven by allowing this cleansing. Jesus is reclaiming the earth. That is a wonderful thing and will ensure that your children's children will not have to contend with the darkness of sin that surrounds your children. It would please Jesus if you would be thankful to Him, despite any circumstances. A saint conducts herself this way and finds that she is joyful regardless of any and all hardships. Dear friends of Heaven, the enemy will not prevail. You know this because you have been told this. At the end of this time, Jesus will return and the earth will be beautiful again. Before that, there will be a time when it will appear that the enemy has taken control of the world. The darkness of sin will reign and our beloved Church will suffer even more. Followers will face grave and constant attacks for their faith in many areas of the world. They will persevere and set the most beautiful example for others. This will draw others back to the faith in great numbers, so you see, the enemy's strategy will backfire. The more God's enemies persecute His children, the more children will choose God and remain true. It has always been this way, sadly. God's children should serve Him faithfully in good times also, but many do not. Many become worldly when the times are easy. Be brave. Your courage will come from Heaven and inspire many. We teach you how to prepare and those who take our advice will find that they are calm and able to lead. Heaven will call upon many to lead because during the worst of the troubles, holy souls will be cut off from each other. Leaders will spring up in every area to help holy souls to remain steadfast. How beautiful are these times when viewed from our perspective. My dear friends, read about our lives. Many saints in Heaven faced the greatest of persecutions on earth. We never relied upon ourselves and in that way we became invincible. You will too. The earth will quake during this time and Heaven's responses will be apparent to all, giving the faithful great hope. The enemy's actions will be met with heavenly retribution. This also will convince many that God is preparing to return and will also bring many back to God. So you see, the enemy cannot win and God will turn everything to the good. It is important that you are aware of the coming events so you will be confident and prepared. My friends, your world is asleep at this time and many doubt God's presence in the world. I would advise you all to remain alert. You will be glad that you did.

July 9, 2004
St. Anthony of Padua

My dear friends in the world, all is well in Heaven, where you will eventually dwell. All is tranquil and graces flow freely from one soul to another, after originating in the Godhead. Truly, we are at peace. With this said, we are also at the alert because we are, like you, awaiting the sweeping changes that will alter the way of life in your world. We are glad for you, dear souls, because the world you have experienced is so unhappy. You do not even realize how difficult it is for you because you cannot compare it to our heavenly vision. Some older souls will remember perhaps that your world was not always filled with such darkness and confusion but for this current generation there is a void in knowledge of goodness. Many youth in the world now have never experienced goodness and peace because there are no souls following Christ near them. Can you imagine how this makes us feel? If there were not changes coming, we would feel helpless. But changes are coming so we feel invigorated and optimistic. We are all committed to working alongside you to bring about changes on the ground, as it were, by which I mean in souls. You may feel you have no control because you did not choose this time and neither will you choose to participate in the events that will usher in the New Time. This is true but I ask you to view it from my perspective. I am one who loved Jesus dearly and served Him as best I could. When I look at the opportunities you have for service to the Kingdom, I am truly jealous in the nicest way. If you are a great artist and you are viewing the work of another great artist, you may say, "I would do that another way." Your vision would be different. At the same time you would admire and respect the work done by your colleague. That is how it is for us. We look with the greatest of respect and admiration at the way you are all dealing with these times. We are always ready with advice or encouragement. Do you understand? We are like soldiers who have faced the very same enemies and enemy strategies. When you get stuck, you must ask us for help, understanding that we view from above, as it were, so can see more clearly what is up ahead of you. In this way we can help you to divert from possible dangers and traps. I am Anthony. I love you dearly and consider you my closest friends. I want only to help you and I continue to thank Jesus for allowing me to communicate with all of you on earth. I am your friend. Talk to me. Allow me to help you. There are many of us and if you have friends in Heaven, you must ask them for help now because they have been given enhanced intercessory powers during this time. We are all going to work together to see you through this transition and the earth will be remarkably beautiful afterwards. All that need concern you is service on each day. Everything else will be cared for by Heaven. Never become discouraged because truly there is no need to be.

July 10, 2004
St. Anthony of Padua

*My brothers and sisters of the world have been
told many things. We have talked about
changes and darkness. We have talked about
persecutions. We have talked about love and
peace and prayer. Today I wish to talk about
death. So many souls on earth fear death.
Dearest souls, destined to come to Heaven, you
should not fear death. It is only through the
death of your body that your soul can come
truly alive. This is something to be anticipated
with joy, not fear. Consider a child in the womb.
Would that child be correct in remaining in the
womb because he feared life? You laugh at
such a notion, yet this is the very same as your
fearing death. He would fear life, perhaps,
because it would be a change for him, and you
fear death because it will be a change for you.
But as you would tell the infant that life is
wonderful, I am telling you that Heaven is
wonderful and the day of your death is truly the
day of your birth because your soul is born
then into eternity. This is a good thing. It is a
joyous thing for anyone who has followed
Christ. All of your faith, all of your sacrifices,
and all of your dutiful acts are justified and
rewarded. Do not walk in fear of death because
it will cause you to cling to life in such a way
that you cannot live freely. You should consider*

that statement if you find it elusive. It is important. I wish to help you to be free of fears so please call on me if you fear death. It will hamper your spirituality so we must eradicate this fear. Children, there will come a time when you will see death in great numbers. Some societies, those who have suffered famine or war, have had this experience. For Christians, this experience changes how one lives. This is good. All experiencing tragic events such as these will realize that they are mortal while they are on earth and that they could be taken at any time. But the true Christian is then encouraged to service because what else is of any value when you could be abruptly called to Heaven? There is no point in storing up earthly treasures if you are only to leave them shortly. Men in affluent areas should also understand this but they do not. There you see a false sense of man controlling his destiny. This creates an environment where souls live for the world. Because they are so busy, they do not give proper consideration to the bigness of reality in comparison to their small little circle of living. They will, my friends, when their circle of living is pierced by hardship and death. I do not say this in gladness, believe me, please. I say this in solemnity. It is all good, though, because it will bring souls back to consideration of God and Heaven and service to God during life. This is what is required and this is what will happen. We will rejoice, you and I, as God ushers in these changes. Be prayerful and silent as often as possible. In this way we can help Jesus to fill you with peace.

Part Two:
Saints—Week Two

July 12, 2004
St. Gertrude the Great

Dear brothers and sisters, how brave you are to read these words with faith. There must be a great push now for detachment. Try to concentrate on heavenly thoughts and heavenly goals, even while you remain in the world. In this way you will detach from the world more effectively and you will see the fruits of these words in your soul. Words are simply words, as you know, until they begin to impact behaviors and habits and, of course, souls. If you ingest these words quietly, they will take root in your souls and all manner of beautiful and exotic blooms will begin to form. The graces are there, my friends. Heaven needs only a willing spirit who will put herself in silence so that these graces can take root. Do not let these graces be wasted. Sometimes souls take the graces and admire their beauty. They correctly assess the worth of these heavenly gifts. But it is one thing to admire the work of a beautiful blanket or quilt. It is another to wrap yourself in it and allow it to warm you, which is its true function. The true function of these words and their accompanying graces is growth. We want to facilitate change in your souls. Your souls must stretch now and to do that you must minimize the attention you pay to the world and maximize the attention you pay to your faith.

Jesus is with you, awaiting your notice so that He can take your hand and begin a walk of union with you. Do not hold back from Him because you limit Him when you do. Give Him everything. Ask Him all throughout the day what you can do for Him. Do this fearlessly, understanding that if He gives you something to do, He will give you every grace necessary to do it. You need fear nothing, little souls. I have the greatest of love and understanding for you, as do we all. We repeat that so you will be reminded and remember to call upon us in your moments of difficulty or fear. Many things can cause fear but usually if you are aligned with Jesus your fears are easily managed. You will know when you are neglecting your prayers, my friends, because fears will begin to creep back into your minds. When I felt fear I began to praise God. In this way I turned the fear into a prayer and trained myself to allow Jesus to eradicate my fears. He always did. Again I say you should ask for the graces as the graces are there. You should not feel that you cannot experience the joy of Jesus because you are afraid. That would tell you that something is wrong and quite possibly you must simply pray more. We speak in simple words because Heaven never seeks to confuse. Confusion does not come from Heaven so you understand that it comes from the enemy of Heaven. Confusion, like fear, is a symptom of the enemy's presence. Expect to struggle with these little crosses at times and you will not be alarmed or pay too much attention. When you find the cross of confusion or fear becoming heavy or quite noticeable, flee to your duty and wrap yourself in prayer. We all carried those crosses, dear friends. We understand and will help you. Suffering from these things does not mean you do not serve Christ well. On the contrary, it would be a nice thing to walk in blissful peace at all times but if you are a follower of Christ this will not be your experience, believe me. I say this with a light heart because we in Heaven are so joyful at the beautiful and brave way that we accepted such crosses. It is like running a race against yourself and winning. We look back and say, "That fear could have distracted me from serving Christ but I kept my eyes on Christ and did not let it. Good for me." You will say this too and you too will be joyful at what you accomplish.

July 13, 2004
St. Gertrude the Great

Dear brothers and sisters, along with detachment you must practice humility. You have words from Heaven, but what will you do with these words? Will you understand that God is calling you to be an apostle? Truly, that is the case. Have you answered that call? You will be first in Heaven, my friends, but you must allow yourself to be last on earth. You have been given great spiritual food, along with many spiritual graces. You will not want to waste these graces by continuing to march to the tune of the enemy. Step out of that group that follows the world and follow us, your heavenly friends. We are humble because we compare ourselves to Christ. Compare yourself to Him and you will also feel humble. When you are humble, He can make you great. It is not hard to understand if you are detached from the world. Heaven is so different. When you consider worldly thinking, just reverse it and often you will find yourself thinking in heavenly terms. I love you very much. We all do. I want you to do well for Jesus' sake, yes, but also for your own sake. My greatest joy in Heaven comes from the knowledge that I served Jesus as best I could, given my many faults, while on earth. Consider in silence what He wants from you and then do it. Do not delay and say you will serve later because He is asking you to

serve now. This is a time of the greatest grace
but it is very much the calm before the storm.
The storm will come, my friends. Of that you
must be certain. Jesus, in all of His mercy, is
prepared to act. We in Heaven are also
prepared. You might say we are all poised. I
know that many of you sense this and you are
correct. Do not become complacent. Also, do
not be fearful. Why would you be? You are at
risk of dying on each and every day you rise
from your rest. What would be worse than
death today would be for you to rise and not
serve Jesus. That is how we think and when you
come to Heaven, and you will, you will also
think like this. Serve during this time of calm.
Spread our words. Offer encouragement to
souls who are seeking truth. Bring truth to
souls who are discouraged in the world and do
not know to seek truth. Commit yourselves to
Christ and let nothing stop you from His
service. I began by talking about humility.
These two concepts are linked in this way. You
are a chosen apostle, but you must be a humble
chosen apostle so that you do not put others off.
If you spend time with Christ each day you will
remain humble. Many convert to Christ and
then feel they are above all of mankind. They
think they have reached sainthood merely by
their altered path. I assure you, little servants,
it is through the ascent that you achieve
sainthood. The higher you climb, the more
humble you will become. Do not hold yourself

above anyone, ever. You will not make friends for Christ this way. You will confirm the enemy's propaganda that Christians hold themselves above others. True Christians, of course, do not. You will know these things by your spirit, but I, Gertrude, am giving you advance warning of a snare that could trip you up. Practice humility. The battle is won in the silence of your soul, my dearest friend. Remember to use us to help you.

July 14, 2004
St. Damien of Molokai

Greetings to my brothers and sisters on earth. I have so much to tell you. I watch your difficulties and understand your struggles. You walk with Jesus, though, and if you remain in an awareness of His presence you will feel stronger and more confident. Many of your struggles can be minimized with constant acts of Holy Indifference. Jesus, along with all of His many helpers, needs you to be His hands, His heart, and His representatives. He can get the work done through you quite easily. You are a part of the work but not the whole work. Let me make this even clearer. If you remain small, understanding that without the help of God you are without power, He can do the greatest things through you. When man swells in his heart and feels that it is he himself who is accomplishing these things, the trouble begins. Egos are difficult friends and dreadful rulers. Keep your ego on a very short leash and understand that your merit lies in your obedience to Christ. Do not take credit for what Christ does through you. He cannot entrust great missions to you if your ego swells with each success. When your work is successful, praise God. When your work fails, praise God. When the sun shines, praise God. When the rain falls, praise God. Do you get the idea? You serve Him and He will do great things through you. These great things have nothing to do with you except that you allowed Heaven to use you as an instrument. Your merit in Heaven will not depend on the greatness of your mission or the greatness of what Christ accomplished through you. Your merit will reflect the work you did in your soul, the policing of your ego, the honing of the virtues, the self-denial, and the love that you allowed to flow through you to other souls. I am trying to prepare you because you are about to see great things happen, brothers and sisters, and I do not want you to swell up with pride and vanity. You will not if you continue to pray and spend time with Jesus. We tell you this for a reason. The risk is present but you will overcome these temptations. When a soul is following Christ during this time, and a soul is committed to the mission of mercy Christ is embarking upon, that soul will be the vehicle for many graces. I do not want my brothers and sisters to fall into the snare of taking credit for what the Savior is doing. This cripples the flow of graces. You are going to see many wonders, my friends. You should remain calm and accept all in a spirit of holiness and humility. The times demand these extraordinary actions of Heaven. There are many conversion powers attached to these words so see that you spread them to the best of your ability, following His lead and direction. Do not hesitate to call on us, your heavenly comrades, to help you in any part of this mission or in any part of your spiritual work. My last word of direction for today is this. Rise each morning and do the work on your soul. That is always your first priority. Spend time in prayer. Be a close friend of Jesus Christ, not only in service, but also in communion of spirit. Then you will be certain that the work is His and not yours. If you notice that you are not praying enough, you will begin to see symptoms. You will take things personally. You will be frightened, anxious, and lose confidence. Those are symptoms that you need to spend more time in prayer. This will be a temptation for you, the apostles of these times, and that is why we, your heavenly friends, are warning you. Walk always in the awareness of the army of saints who march beside you.

July 15, 2004
St. Damien of Molokai

My brothers and sisters, you are serving Jesus and that should give you the greatest joy. There is nothing more important than saying "yes" to Him each day and stepping out in faith. You do not even realize the many ways in which He uses you during the day. That is as it should be when you are a servant. I found that my greatest strength lay in my practice of remaining in the present. I never panicked because I did not worry about the future. It was enough for me to serve Christ in the moment, in each poor little soul He placed in my path. The more you serve, the greater joy in the service. Some of you have found this already. One becomes a better climber when one has been climbing and the path to Heaven, regardless of the difficulty, becomes simply a day's work. What beautiful servants Jesus relies on today. There will be an army of servants for you to work with very soon because Jesus is calling many and sending great graces to enable souls to hear His call. Many will serve during this time and souls will be saved. Please, my friend, put Jesus first each moment. This is not a time for half-hearted commitments. This is a time for dying to self and living for Jesus completely. If you begin this journey at all you will see what He can do through you if you are willing to allow Him to work. With your ego firmly under control, you will marvel at the goodness of Jesus and the preparation He has given you without your being aware. Use your every skill, your every strength, and serve the Kingdom. We will all help you, as we keep reminding you. You will call on our help and we would like to put you into the habit of doing so quickly, so it will be second nature to you when difficulties come. Brothers and sisters, the time of darkness is over, it is true. But the enemy is not finished yet. He rallies souls to his service to persecute the children of Mary. He seeks to erase God from God's world. This is the process you are witnessing, except now you see souls fighting back. Heaven's children are waking up and shaking off the lethargy that overcame them. So now the battles begin in earnest. So be it. Heaven is ready. You are ready. God will have His world back and His children will be safe again, but not without the struggle, which is what we are preparing you for through these words. Children of God, it will become clear that souls are choosing sides in that souls following the enemy will persecute God's followers and delight in doing so. It has never been God's way to extract revenge for the sake of revenge, or to allow His children to do so. You will be called upon to answer in love. There are a great many readers pausing, I see. This is difficult, I know. I had my share of enemies on earth and this was difficult for me, particularly when I was being castigated for doing good in a time when few were willing to assist me. Their response was to slander me. I tell you this so you know that I understand what I am saying to you and I understand that it will be a great Christian challenge. But we, the saints, lived for these challenges and so must you. Do not fear that you will not serve. You will make mistakes, as I did, but generally Jesus will use you successfully to further His will. Love your enemy. That is the message and that has always been His message. I will help you.

July 16, 2004
St. Matthew the Apostle

I send my greetings to my brothers and sisters on earth. I am happy to be speaking to you and look forward to greeting you here in Heaven when your time on earth is finished. How quickly it goes by, dear friends. Do not worry about suffering because it is truly brief, even if it lasts for a lifetime. I have come to do my part in enlightening you. You are given this extra help because you have been given extra challenges in that you participate in a time of great trouble. There is also great joy available, as you well know, and true followers will find these times invigorating. The smaller and more humble you become, the greater the flow of graces that can flow through you into the world. Jesus is grateful to you. You know that. Call as many servants into the fold as you can. Do not be afraid to tell souls that Jesus needs their help. You must encourage others to take up their crosses and follow because more workers will complete the tasks more quickly and easily. These are all obvious pieces of advice. I want to speak to you now about something that is less obvious. Brothers and sisters, and may I say dear friends, there will come a time when the choice between Jesus and the world will cost you something. During that time, many families will split because many souls will say, "Yes, I will serve, but not unto death and not at the cost of my comfort and well-being." But for you...what is He asking of you? Is He asking you to serve a little bit? Does He want to possess a part of you, leaving the remainder to the world? Did Jesus Christ stop cold at the foot of Calvary and say, "I want to love these souls, yes, but not unto death?" No, my friends. Jesus Christ ascended Calvary and finished the job of redemption. It cost Him something. It cost Him everything. But He persevered. So what do you think He is asking of you?

You must give with entirety. You must make the decision now and never divert, regardless of the cost. There will come a time when families will split. This will cause you pain, my friend, it is true. But you will not divert. You are not called upon to divert. You are chosen as an apostle of these days to complete the mission our great God has entrusted to you. You may have glimpsed your mission and you may be on your path but there are many things yet to come. I am Matthew. I love you dearly and congratulate you on your service to this God of All. Understand that when the division comes you will be filled with graces and you who have decided for Christ will have no decision at all. You will ascend Calvary with Him and join us as loyal friends of the Savior. Be at peace in all of this. God will hear your prayers for your families. We tell you these things so that you will embrace your mission with the appropriate seriousness. We will not abandon you during the difficult times. You will have these words of truth, truly, from which graces will flow unchecked. You will have our companionship, also, through many prophets. And you will have joy in those days, dear friends. You will have joy.

July 17, 2004
St. Matthew the Apostle

Brothers and sisters, I have come with words of encouragement for you. The words and thoughts in these messages are an example of the great mercy of our God in Heaven. You will be so grateful that you served when you are called to come home. There is no regret like the regret you will have if you say "no" to Jesus during this time. We know Jesus, both as man and as God. He is all love. He is all kindness. He is all encouraging and uplifting. Jesus never leaves you feeling saddened, unless you are walking away without determination to serve Him. Spend time with Him always because you will always feel refreshed and determined. I got all of my courage from Jesus Christ personally, whether I was in His presence or not. Truly, I felt united to Him because I allowed Him to be united to me. You can do that, too. That is one of the opportunities you have during these days especially. Jesus wants to work through you. To do that, He must be with you. Would you like to walk with Christ, constantly united to Him and in His presence? You can. Just make the decision and ask Him to be with you. Then, when you have done that, do not ignore Him or treat Him with such familiarity that you forget Him. He is your closest friend. He is your ever-

present advisor. Think of your current problems. What does Jesus say about these problems? What is His opinion? What does He want you to do about these struggles or conflicts? If you do not know the answer, you are not doing it right. Spend time in silence with Him and ask Him. I lived like this. All day long I said, "Jesus, what would You like me to do? Jesus, how are You going to handle this?" He will give you the answer and you will reach His goal of behaving as another Christ in the world. Brothers and sisters, we do not wish to bore you by repeating lessons. But because we are also experienced with humanity, we know that often you must learn the same lessons over and over. Repetition and practice bring perfection. We know that. We learned it the old-fashioned way which was by making the same mistakes and relearning these important lessons. Jesus is with you. Jesus will never leave you. Do not be afraid and do not make any decisions without His counsel. If you are fearful, you are doing something wrong. If you are panicking, you are doing something wrong. If you feel dislike for most of your brothers and sisters, you are doing something wrong. And if you feel you are better than most of your fellow apostles, you are in trouble. I am making a joke so do not be too serious. I speak of such serious things that I feel I must lighten your mood. In all of this, you should feel a sense of liberation because when Jesus is leading your life you are liberated. Can you imagine the burden of doing it all by yourself? Imagine the fear of making mistakes if you put yourself back in charge. Truly, once you begin walking with Christ it would be very traumatic to break away on your own again. The world would once again become the frightening place it is for non-believers. I love you so passionately, my friends. We all do. We are so eager to help you. We can give you the most beautiful counsel. Talk to us often and we will find ways to help you and obtain beautiful gifts of grace from our God. Peace be with you, dear fellow apostles. You are in the greatest of company.

Part Three:
Saints—Week Three

July 19, 2004
St. Christopher
(An Unknown Saint)

*I send heartfelt greetings to all of my brothers
and sisters on earth. I pray that you will thank
God often for these beautiful graces. Souls
embracing these words understand how great a
gift is offered to the world in these humble little
Volumes. We in Heaven thank Him constantly,
all the while asking for even greater and more
numerous gifts of grace for you. Earthly souls,
we understand how difficult it can be to serve
steadily while you are in a body that is
demanding from you constantly. Practice
disciplining your body. Say "no" to your body
on occasion so that your body will understand
that your soul is in charge. If your body is
directing, your soul will not be honored as
much as it should be. For your soul to breathe,
to grow, and to flourish, your body must be
disciplined. Fasting is a good way to let your
body understand that it is not in charge. When
you fast you deny your body and nourish your
soul. Your soul grows strong and confident
during these periods. The enemy becomes weak
and ineffectual in your life if you are fasting.
Can I ask that you take two days in each week
and give up a little something that your body
would like to have? You do not have to begin
with a strict fast and if you are not used to*

51

fasting I do not encourage you to do so. Begin small, with little sacrifices. Keep busy and do not think about your body. Think about Jesus, Heaven, our beautiful Blessed Mother, angels, and what you would like to discuss with us, your heavenly friends, when you arrive here. Think of the questions you have for Jesus. Think of what you would like to learn about when you arrive in Heaven. Think about the beauty of participating in a worldwide mission of mercy. That is what you are doing, you know. You have become part of Christ's team and we are working together to save many souls before the changes come. What an honor is yours, my friend, that Jesus is calling you in this way. Do not think about your body. Treat it with respect and dignity, caring for its needs, but do not spoil your body. Rest, take nourishment, exercise your body. Jesus is not asking for rigorous fasts or penances. But He would be greatly pleased with a little self-denial. Fast for Heaven. Fast for Jesus. Fast for the dreadful unhappiness and emptiness so prevalent in your world. If you attempt to fast and you fail to reach your goal, be forgiving of yourself and try again on another day. Be at peace in everything but do try. I am trying to enter you into spiritual training. We want you to be gentle in spirit, but also tough in your ability to serve Christ. Spend little time worrying about how you compare to others. Just serve. Work on your own little soul in the life where Jesus has placed you. You need to keep the big view in mind, of course, but not so much that you begin to neglect your vocational duties, such as your families. Some think they should serve Christ in blazing glory when they are called to serve in humble quietness. If you are called to serve in blazing glory, you will know, believe me. Otherwise, care for your duties in obscurity and gladness. Your quiet little acts of love and self-denial will propel this mission to completion. I love you all. You will come to know many saints in the days to come. Saints are simply people who are finished on earth and who have fought the good fight. As such, we are experienced soldiers and now come to support you, our brothers and sisters.

July 19, 2004
St. Christopher
(An Unknown Saint)

My brothers and sisters in the world give God the greatest glory in their faith. Your world has become cynical and mistrusting. It is fashionable to be skeptical and to question the motives of anyone who works for good. I see that this skepticism has spread even into holy circles and into groups of servants who formerly would have renounced skepticism. I am referring to priests and religious, actually, but not exclusively. If you are a consecrated servant of Jesus Christ, you should not be cynical. If you are cynical, you need to examine where you are spending most of your time. Spend more time with Jesus and less in the world and you will lose this symptom of despair. It will be replaced by joyful hope and a willingness to assume that each member of humanity has the capacity for great goodness. Worldly souls will then call you an innocent. Well, dear friends, if you are a holy soul, you are supposed to be an innocent. Saintly souls are childlike. Children are innocent. This is a good thing. Do you understand? Be joyful. Be innocent. And be holy enough to realize that the earth and everything in it is God's beautiful creation, which He created to serve Him in goodness. Do not be embarrassed by your innocence. Attempt to spread this joyful attitude of trust in the Savior. Other souls will see it, you can be sure, and they will then examine their own attitudes. They need to do this if they are cynical and skeptical in the latest way of the world.

Brothers and sisters, this new sophistication is not from God. It is really hurt. Souls see that things are not what they should be. They do not understand why this is so and they adapt this attitude as a protection. They then embrace it and it becomes an opportunity to ridicule all that is truly good. But at its source it is still hurt. This will spread, if you can believe that. It will become more pronounced. What will this mean to you, God's little ones? Well first of all, as we said, you will stand out even further. Secondly, it will be more of a challenge for you to retain your hopeful innocence. You will receive great graces, it is true, but you will stand out. The good part about standing out in your joy and hope is that other souls will reject this complete and total attitude of sophisticated scorn. They will be drawn to you because of your joy and they will correctly suspect that you hold the truth. They will join you. Do you see that God brings everything to the good? You must believe that with your whole heart and you will have peace. It is truth. I am God's chosen servant and I speak only the truth. You will be like me, speaking truth in your world.

God will bring good from everything. We are all here to help you. Ask me for help and I will begin immediately to intercede for you. All is well. We are merely giving you advance warning of the coming times. If you look closely, you will see that God has always done this. Some souls receive the words and some reject them. Again, this is not different. Trust us and most of all trust Jesus.

July 20, 2004
St. Julia Ursula Ledochowska

Hello to all of my brothers and sisters on earth. I am so happy to speak with you so directly. We speak to you indirectly all of the time, even though you are not aware of it. We prompt you, console you, and place great truths in your hearts, particularly when you are struggling. During this time God has willed that we speak to you clearly, as in an earthly letter. He chose this soul to record for Him and we send our words through her. He is very good to allow this because, while there are always prophets, this body of work is very large and will be very complete. Certainly the times have called for heavenly assistance. My friends, we are trying to encourage you to live for Jesus and His holy will. Many are doing this beautifully and you are seeing how He works through you. This is the encouragement that fuels further cooperation, of course. Be steadfast now. You have made your decision for Jesus and now you must awaken each day and remind yourself that you are His slave. Give Him your day each morning and relinquish your will to Him. Move through your day then with the awareness that He is using you to do His work. Perhaps He is using you to clean your house in a spirit of unity to Him. In this way He extracts great graces from your cooperation, which He then uses to save souls. Maybe He has put you in the world. In that way He is using you to be a witness to Him, even though you may never mention His name. Your Christian ways are your witness and, truly, you bring Him into each room and meeting and situation. Maybe you do manual work. Unite it to Jesus and He can spend the whole day with you, perhaps resting in your welcoming soul and drawing great consolations from your love for Him. This softens His just wrath in the most beautiful fashion. Each one of you, regardless of your tasks and roles, is called upon to live for Jesus. Those of you who suffer illness should be especially aware of your ability to console the Savior. He will never leave you. He will use each pain, each limitation, each frustration as a balm to His wounds if you allow Him. Imagine being able to apply a beautiful healing balm to the wounds of the Savior. Truly, you can, by unit-ing hardship and illness to Jesus. If you think of it in that way you will think less of being released from hardships and more of utilizing your hardships for Heaven. Brothers and sisters, you know that we want to help you. You know that we love you. There are many of us who are especially chosen to assist you during this time. It would be good for you to develop your relationships with us now, during this quiet time before the storm. If you are well trained spiritually you will respond efficiently to anything that comes your way. Each region will see different changes, of course, and each soul will have specific help for his experiences. Receive every life experience as something directly from the hands of our Jesus and you will not object. Try that today. Each situation that occurs in your life is directly from Jesus. He wants to teach you something. He wants to introduce you to someone's suffering, perhaps to encourage you to become more prayerful. He wants to draw you further into His heart, or perhaps He wants to teach you patience. Do this with me today. I am Julie and I want to help you to see each and every event in your day as an opportunity to perfect your soul. Allow me to do this for you. Speak to me often today. Ask me what Jesus is trying to teach you and I will tell you. Consider this exercise as practice in learning to work with us, your heavenly guides. You know we are here. You know we want to help you. This is how we are going to do it. Let us begin.

July 21, 2004
St. Julia Ursula Ledochowska

Brothers and sisters, I await your petitions. When you ask a saint for help, that saint immediately turns to the throne and begins to pray for you. She brings your trouble or question directly to God and requests the graces to assist you. God enjoys the relationships between his children because it is another manifestation of love, which always originates from Him. You see, if you spy one of your earthly siblings in trouble, and you move to help them, that is love. Well, my dear brothers and sisters, it is the same way. Your parents, generally speaking, would applaud you for helping your sibling. Our God is the same. We please Him greatly when we go to the Throne and beg for graces for you. He likes to see us working together. When we have served Him well on earth, His heart is very soft toward us and we can move Him to all manner of mercies. Can you go directly to Jesus? Of course you can. You should always be with Jesus and take your cares to Him. There are times, though, you will see, when you would like our input and we will be there for you.

There will come a time when the world will seem very dark. You will have little hope that God is going to turn it around and allow His grace to take the earth back. My friends, during this time you will use us. God does everything for the good of His people and it will be important to remember that during the times to come. I do not seek to frighten you but in the eyes of non-faithful souls it will seem as though God wreaks vengeance. In your eyes it will seem that God has forgotten you. In the eyes of Heaven, the truth will be that God is preparing to return. The darkest hour truly can come before the dawn and it will be that way during the time of transition. We, Heaven's saints, will be active and aggressive for our kindred spirits on the earth. You will ask us for help. You will get it. We will secure great courage for you. We will help you maintain your faith and your hope. We will even help you with practical matters on occasion. You see that you are being prepared. Well, we are preparing the world, as it were, and not just one soul. And yet we are personally preparing your precious soul. My dearest comrades, you need to do this anyway. Your death could come today and you will be finished. We are simply telling you that your world is going to change. Look closely at your world. Could this possibly be a bad thing? If you think it is, you are not looking with the eyes of Jesus because He is not pleased at the situation in your world today. No, we cannot speak an untruth. Jesus is not pleased. That statement carries the heaviest of weights with it. Truly, all of the anchors in the world could not compare to the weight of that statement. Jesus is not pleased. Your time on earth is limited, regardless of what occurs. Use it to serve.

July 22, 2004
St. Daniel Comboni

We are happy for you, my brothers and sisters. The time of darkness is both nearing its end and drawing nearer. The difference between the darkness of past times is that in the past you experienced the darkness of sin. The future darkness will be the darkness of purification. Of the two, I would anticipate the latter with greater joy. This is obvious because whatever comes from God's hand is for our benefit, whereas anything that comes from the hand of the enemy will work against us and pull us away from truth. So when you consider the future and you feel the very human impulse to be afraid, remember that God is directing the changes. You cannot fear what comes from God because He will use it for your sanctification. Let us consider sanctification. Sanctification is a process, rather than an event or a state of being. We move through this process obtaining greater and greater spiritual abilities and awareness. We are destined to reach a certain level on the earth. We do this through cooperation with Christ's sanctifying grace, which we are granted through prayer, the sacraments, and generally living life as a Christian. Now, my friends on earth will not be offended if I say that from my vantage point, the high ground that is Heaven, I see a world in which many, including many who were destined to be great spiritual leaders, have failed to cooperate with the process of sanctification in their lives. This is bad. The world suffers, souls directly around this person who were destined to flourish, whither, and the individual himself does not reach the high level that is available to him. This widespread phenomenon of "non serviam" is a result of the darkness, of course, but has also fueled the darkness. I speak now of the darkness of sin and not the darkness of purification. After the darkness of purification, which is allowed by God, souls will serve again. They will cooperate joyfully with the process of sanctification in their lives. Brothers and sisters, there will be peace on earth. That will be the end result. Of course, like sanctification, there is a process necessary to get from here to there. The upheavals in your world are that process. It will look like an extended and inflated time of the enemy's darkness but I am telling you today that our Lord, in His wisdom and mercy, is allowing the enemy to run, knowing full well that the enemy, evil in your world, cannot survive. You are familiar with the idea of giving a bad person enough rope with which he eventually does damage to himself? That is a general description of what is to occur. For those of you who object to this, tempted toward anger at God for allowing the enemy to operate, let me say that you are shouting a little too late and a little too softly. Please remember that if humanity had been obedient, the world would not have gotten to this point. Now do not be angry at me for speaking the truth. Surely even in your own life you will see that there were times when you did not cooperate with Christ. Few in this time have truly cooperated. Am I trying to insult you and make enemies? No. I am also a great sinner so if you keep company with me you will be in the company of a reformed sinner. I do not hide my flaws because it is through the conquering of them that I was sanctified. I am your friend. Call on me to help you. When you are tempted to sin, cry out, "Daniel, I need graces." I will get them for you and you will be triumphant. Do not fear the future. It is God's time.

July 24, 2004
St. Daniel Comboni

My brothers and sisters have difficulty separating from their earthly lives. You must begin to see your soul as a separate entity from this world. Your body, your life here, these are the vehicles with which your soul is sanctified. So your life is really a means to an end. You are here to gain eternity. You are here to serve God during your exile from Heaven. You have been told you are to earn Heaven here and that is true. But dear friends, let me assure you, having been in both places, we, none of us, merit Heaven. When you live for Christ, earth is a joyful place to be. When you serve Christ on earth and come to Heaven? There are no words. I cannot convey it to you except to say that every one of your greatest, most beyond belief hopes for Heaven will be satisfied and your experience here will so far exceed that expectation that you will not believe you ever harbored hopes so low. Imagine being able to fly with no assistance except your will. You could fly as high, as low, as fast, as slow, and as often as you liked. You could go anywhere. The wind on your face would fill you with rejoicing. You would laugh aloud for the joy of it. You would delight in the joy of others who also experienced this perfect ability. Imagine never feeling too cold or too hot. Always you feel perfectly balanced with the elements, unless you suddenly crave warmth or cold. Then it is there for your enjoyment. I am probably making a mistake by trying to convey to you the smallest portion of Heaven because it is impossible. Yet I feel I must give you some idea of why you are to be selfless for a small time. Imagine being with the people you loved, but always with the most perfect understanding of each other. What adventures you will share. Dear brothers and sisters, never worry about death. Please. Death is the greatest liberation you can imagine. God has the day of your death already established. It will come. And you will be ready if you serve Christ. You will have no regrets. You would not want to surrender your body to Jesus and feel as though you missed the whole point of your life. Serve, my beloved friends. Serve. Serve Jesus. Serve each other. Serve strangers. Serve. The last shall be first. Do not seek to be bigger than your earthly companions. Do not seek earthly respect and homage. Seek only to serve and through your service you will perfect your precious soul, which will join me here. We will greet you, you can be assured. We will rejoice in your coming and you will thank us for these words, particularly if you take them to your heart and let them change you. In these words you will find the greatest of wisdom. You will see that. You will not see the graces that flow from these words into your souls and through your actions for others. But you will discern the graces by a new reflective quiet. You will consider your eternity and what you would like to do to prepare for it. You have been given this day, or rather this moment. Do you know for certain that you will see the end of this day? You do not. Perhaps this moment, these next few moments, will be your last opportunity to claim something for Jesus. This is how you are to live each day. In this way you will serve. You will not change immediately. Do not expect this. Remember that sanctification is a process. But you can immediately make the decision to change and begin the process. I am giving you good advice. A wise man accepts good counsel. Be wise. Serve.

Part Four:
Saints—Week Four

July 26, 2004
St. Catherine of Siena

I send greetings to my brothers and sisters who struggle so valiantly for Jesus. I am with you. We, your brothers and sisters in Heaven, know your struggles well. You will not encounter anything for the first time in this heavenly family. There is always someone who faced a similar struggle. Call out for help, my brothers and sisters. Use Heaven. Use your friends in Heaven. Ask for new friends in Heaven if you encounter something and you do not know of anyone here who has faced that struggle. You will get immediate intervention and assistance. You may not see us standing next to you, but we are there. There are different states of awareness and generally speaking those on earth, in their bodies, do not see heavenly beings. You just do not have the eyes for that vision. On occasion, when it suits Heaven's purposes, earthly souls are given heavenly eyes temporarily so that they can convey messages or be strengthened or simply draw attention to Heaven and God. Those souls have a difficult time because they are not brought immediately to Heaven, but must finish their work. They can get very lonesome. Do not wish for this type of experience because it is actually a cross in many ways and there are great obligations that accompany it. You will have crosses enough without seeking new ones or additional ones. Embrace the crosses Jesus has placed with you. Often souls think they would do better with a different cross. Usually this is a form of rejecting the job Jesus has given you. Remember that Jesus has given you exactly the cross or crosses that will perfect your precious little soul. There is work to be done in your soul, of course. You know this. If there were no work to be done, Jesus would have brought you home. So while you are on earth, with work to be done on your soul, work. We always tell you to serve. You might tire of us repeating ourselves and you might think we have nothing new to say or that we are very dreary in our outlook. But my dearest, most beloved friends, we tell you that because we want you to do well and we want to enjoy this wonderful Heaven with as many of you as possible. We know that through service to others and through service to Jesus, you will grow stronger and stronger. The enemy will not be able to divert you from your path to Jesus and by walking that path you will pull many in behind you. You might not believe this, thinking you are not that important, but I assure you that through even the quietest, most humble service, Jesus can save many souls. Look at St. Therese, God's Little Flower. She was not famous. She was not wealthy or powerful. She was obscure. She served God in the smallest, most humble things. Yet she has helped to save many souls and she has only begun her work. I am Catherine of Siena. I have also been allowed to assist with the salvation of many. We are Jesus' helpers. We are here to help you also. Join us because we are very strong. You must live in your world, understanding that you have many friends who are also in your world assisting you. You have an invisible army to assist you. This should make you very strong and courageous indeed. One word of caution for you, dear brothers and sisters. Our goals are not the goals of your world. Our ways are not the ways of the world. We serve Christ. Our wills always reflect the Divine Will. Come now. Work for Heaven as though you have only the smallest time left. You will not regret any sacrifices you make for Him. Please serve.

July 27, 2004
St. Catherine of Siena

My dear brothers and sisters in the world must put all of their hope and trust in Jesus. Souls in the world will fail you, my friends. This is the sad truth. How could they not when they are human and dealing with human weaknesses? Do not be alarmed when this happens to you. I will tell you a secret. You have heard that saints welcomed situations such as this. Do you know why? Because we considered it practice. That was our secret. We knew very well that all trust and hope had to lie with our Jesus. Our goal was to belong totally to Him. When dear friends betrayed us or loved ones failed us, we used the situations as priceless opportunities to grow deeper in unity with Jesus by detaching further from the world, and also to practice His beautiful example of forgiveness. We knew that our time on earth was limited, therefore the opportunities finite. It is important, in that respect, not to let them slip by you without boosting your spiritual growth. So from now on, when you are having difficulties with other souls, thank Jesus. Continually work on your own soul and ask yourself what this opportunity could help you with spiritually. Should you practice humility? Are you too fond of the esteem of others? Should you practice detachment? Is the world an alluring pull for you? Should you practice trust? Are you having difficulty trusting Jesus? Are you seeking to fill your needs through other avenues? My brothers and sisters, that is the tip of the surface, as you know, of spiritual exercising. There is great concern in your world with physical fitness. Well, you are followers of Jesus so let us now spread a great obsession with spiritual fitness. You are being insulted? Consider your prayers exercises to strengthen your detachment from the opinions of others. You are not as successful as you think you should be? This is an opportunity to practice Holy Indifference, which helps you to work for Jesus and not for the results you, in your flawed humanity, desire. Only Jesus knows what results He is trying to achieve. It is not your worry, dear friend. Let it rest with Heaven and continue to serve. Oh, we understand your struggles. We failed many times when we were on earth, but there were those little triumphs as well and great growth came from those moments when we overcame ourselves and served Heaven. You will be fine, my friends. We love you and applaud your efforts. I know there are a great many things to distract you and I know you have a great many concerns, but please, do not let the enemy distract you from growing in your relationship to Jesus and growing in your service to Jesus. This is a time for grace. This is a time for spiritual growth. There are great spiritual opportunities available now. Use every one. We will be with you. We will show you how. It is good to read about us, the saints who have burned trails in holiness. We always looked to other holy ones for example because we wanted to do well for Jesus. Examples are so valuable, are they not? Now, be brave in your day and do not overlook any opportunities for holiness.

July 28, 2004
St. Thomas Aquinas

I send my most respectful greetings to you, the souls serving in the world during this time. I have great respect for you because the battle being waged is without boundaries. The enemy has infiltrated every level of human existence on the earth. There is little sacred anymore and you may look for renewed efforts against God Himself, in the Sacrament of the Eucharist. Truly, the tabernacle houses the Savior, our Redeemer and Creator. This is a sublime mercy that cannot be fully understood while you walk the earth. Those who adore the Eucharist have an inkling of Its power. Jesus transmits many choice graces during Adoration. Adoration of the Blessed Sacrament is our secret weapon. Brothers and sisters, we must spread Adoration throughout the world. I will help you to do this. Look into your life and begin by making a decision to adore Jesus in the Eucharist. Then I ask that you consider how He is asking you to spread this practice. There is something for you to do in this regard and you must ask Him what He requires of you. Graces flow down into the world through these heavenly ports and we must have as many as possible. Those who come to spend time with Jesus are receptacles of this heavenly grace, which they bring into the world for Him. Dearest brothers and sisters, never underestimate what Jesus can do with a soul who decides for Him. To underestimate what He can do is to limit Him. A soul deciding for Jesus can change the world and that is our goal. We must help Him to change this world. You have been given some ideas of the weapons you have at your disposal. You have Jesus, of course. You have Mary. Many also underestimate the power of our Heavenly Mother. Be assured that the enemy knows her power. Do not let your Heavenly Mother be attacked without response. If you witness this, you must speak out for her. This pleases everyone in Heaven, but this pleases Jesus in a special way. She is a loyal friend to you and a powerful intercessor. There are many mercies and graces given to your world today which would be absent but for Mary. We love her immeasurably. You will not err if you follow her. She leads to Jesus. Now, you have been given sound advice and you have been given many warnings. It can be difficult to take all of this in, my friends. It requires time and contemplation. You cannot simply take these words, read them, and expect to be the saint you are intended to be. You have to take these words, follow their advice, and allow Jesus to change you. I am going to ask that each one of you spend time in Adoration because it is there, in silence, that you will understand the gravity of the call that is coming to you. Make this a priority in your life. If you cannot do this, find a quiet time each day to be with Jesus. Ask Him to clarify your role in His Kingdom. Be grateful if your role is small. Be grateful if your role is big. Remember that the heavenly perspective is far different than the earthly perspective. Most of all, you must give Jesus your day. We are with you. We love you. And we will help you.

July 29, 2004
St. Thomas Aquinas

I am grateful to God for His unfailing and limitless mercy in allowing me to speak with you. Can you imagine how grateful I am, dear brothers and sisters? I have watched events in the world, shaking my head at times. The opportunity to speak to you is indeed very precious to me and to each saint who communicates in this way during this time. Friends, you must keep your eyes open and remain alert. Your faith, your God, is being attacked. There is nothing more precious than your faith. Nothing. Through your faith you will inherit your eternity. Man can take everything from you in this world and it will mean nothing because quickly you will leave this world and truly begin to live forever in Heaven. You will not mourn the loss of your earthly possessions. You will count them as nothings. What you will be most interested in is your response to the loss of your earthly possessions. If you respond in bitterness to God, you will be disappointed. What will give you joy is your faithfulness to God. Stay alert. In situations where your God is being attacked, you must respond. We will help you. You should not respond in anger, although you may be angered. If you are prayerful, you will know exactly what our Lord wishes you to do. We are involved in a spiritual war, dear brothers and sisters, and you are the soldiers. There is no choice involved, in the sense that the situation will deteriorate even further. If you are a follower of Jesus Christ, you will be engaged in the war. Jesus requires your help now and you do not want to disappoint Him. If you believe anything at all, believe that statement. You will not want to disappoint Jesus.

My brothers and sisters, you understand that we come to advise you, but also to prepare you, and indeed to advise you on how to prepare. There will come a time when you may be deprived of the Sacrament of the Eucharist altogether. This will occur in some areas of the world. This will be a grave and heavy cross but I assure you that Heaven will compensate. You will make constant spiritual communions and remain united to Christ. You will have angels and saints all around you, willing to console and direct you. You will be very brave and very fixated on your Jesus and on your mission to serve Him. So even in removing the Eucharist, the enemy can do you no real harm. Do you understand? The enemy cannot remove God from you. He cannot do this. He cannot touch your soul. He cannot deprive you of union with Jesus. He is powerless in this regard and you have all the powers of Heaven at your call. Truly, who is the more powerful? You must understand if this happens to you, in your area, that this was foretold and that this moves you closer to the glorious return of the King of Kings.

July 30, 2004
St. Ignatius of Loyola

We have many things to talk about, dear brothers and sisters, but only some of them will be communicated in this way. The other things we want to tell about will be communicated to you in more conventional ways. Many of us have written works of spiritual significance. Those works sometimes chronicle our struggles, which will interest you, I know, but also you can look for the revelations given to us by God. There is a great body of heavenly wisdom on the earth right now. Look to this body of work for deeper knowledge of Jesus and everything to do with God. If you are following these words, you will be interested to read about us and our own difficulties. You will then understand that you are not the first person who has had to suffer for the faith. And you will also understand that when we tell you to trust, we understand that it can require a heroic act of your will. We do not speak lightly to you, my friends. We speak with all gravity, all consideration, and in complete cooperation with God's goals for this mission. So you cannot err if you follow our words. Our words are one with God, because they come from Him and from unity to Him. We are a heavenly family, all together, all joined. You are part of that family, only you are still earning your salvation. Would we return to work for Jesus again, leaving Heaven, with all of its wonders and comforts? Of course we would. It might be difficult to leave Heaven, particularly after knowing Him in this complete sense, but it is for that reason especially that we would sacrifice again. We would do anything for Him and I say that with no reluctance, no hesitations. Truly, when you are with Jesus, you will feel the same. The achievement which we are trying to inspire you to work for is to serve Him completely before you know Him completely. This, your challenge, is done through your faith, your love, your knowledge of Him obtained in contemplation. This knowledge of Him is His gift to you, but He cannot gift you with these graces if you do not want them and if you choose not to accept Him. You must be available to Him in order for Him to work in your soul. Many reject Him now. That is simply the unpleasant truth. We would not hide the truth from you because it is for the truth we have come to you. You will need to use the truth as a weapon. When someone speaks the truth, people listen. They may become angry, they may deny the truth, and they may then try to hide the truth, but they will hear you. And then they must make a choice. You see, my brothers and sisters, there are souls to whom the truth has not been adequately represented. You will change that. We will show you how. One way is to spread these words and to assist those who have accepted the mission of spreading these words. These words are truth. They will spread. But if you can help, you should help. Your reward will be great and you will be part of our team. I am Ignatius. I wish to help you all. Do not be afraid. If you have a heavenly concept that confuses you, ask for my help. I will bring you the information you require. Do not think that heavenly learning is for great scholars. Most saints were not great scholars. Most were simple people who loved God. Try for that. Try to be simple. Try to love God. I love you most tenderly, my friend.

July 30, 2004
St. Ignatius of Loyola

My dear brothers and sisters, I feel such joy in this work. I hope I can transmit some of my joy to you. I am joyful for many reasons. First, I am joyful to be with God and to know that I have completed my time on earth in love for Him. This brings me joy. I am also joyful because God is allowing me to work with you in this mission of mercy to the world. God intends to allow many graces to fall from Heaven. We, His chosen saints, will be responsible for delivering many of these graces. It is for this reason we keep telling you to ask us for help. We have many graces at our disposal and if they run out, He will replenish them. They are a bottomless sack, so to speak, so the more we use, the more we can obtain. Ask, ask, ask. I am joyful because the time of darkness on the earth nears its end. We love you very much. Think of your most beloved friend on the earth. This can be a family member, a parent, a child, a spouse, or a fellow worker. You want the best for that person. When you see him make a mistake you are saddened and grieved. But you do not stop loving him. Indeed, you wish him well and try to find a way to explain to him that he has made a mistake and that while he may be in a fog, you can see clearly how he should avoid

97

We have made your mistakes, we have accomplished your goals, and we have achieved Heaven. Now we want to help you. The fact that Jesus has allowed us such latitude is exciting to us because we can help you in ways we normally could not. Imagine how we are yearning to begin. But you must ask. Some prayers must originate on earth and the graces we have at our disposal, for the most part, must be granted in response to your prayers and requests. Please. Begin to request our help. Now do not be like children asking for new bicycles when you do not need new bicycles. I tease you a little here, my friends, but you understand. Do not ask for worldly things that Jesus may consider bad for you. But, because we are your friends, we do not judge you. So do ask and if you are asking for something inappropriate, you will know because we will gently convey disapproval at your request. You will not, though. You will ask for help in matters that are important to you. You will ask for help in your work, your finances, and your families. And we will help. Brothers and sisters, ask us please to help you to obtain spiritual gains. This pleases all of Heaven. So you must say, "Ignatius, I do not understand how I can work so hard and not care about the outcome of my labors." I will assist you. I will help you to understand why God often allows you to work with little reward. It is the work that is molding your soul, my friend, not the reward. You are working to become better, or stronger, or simply to be God's worker. God's workers are needed everywhere. Many of God's most holy workers spent their lives doing things like sweeping floors and cleaning after others. They were servants on earth. You must believe that they are princes and princesses in the Heavenly Kingdom. So work in joy. Have joy in your work. I love you. Your Heavenly Mother Mary loves you. All of your brothers and sisters here in Heaven love you. God loves you. And we all want to help you.

Appendix

Have you been blessed by reading this book? Please help others receive these words by donating to Direction for Our Times. We are a registered 501(c)3 not for profit organization in the United States and all donations are tax deductible. In Ireland we are a Registered Charity CHY17298.

We are a small organization with a big mission. Your donation makes all the difference. Monthly or one time donations are gratefully accepted.

In Ireland:
Direction For Our Times
The Hague Building
Cullies
Cavan
County Cavan

In the USA:
Direction For Our Times
9000 West 81st Street
Justice, Illinois 60458

+353-(0)49-437-3040
contactus@dfot.ie

708-496-9300
contactus@directionfor
ourtimes.org

Registered Charity CHY17298   A 501(c)(3) Organization

Adult Faith Formation

We are currently offering Adult Faith Formation programs. Please check our website for our most recent events including weekend retreats and our annual School of Holiness held each summer in Ireland. To learn more about these programs please contact one of our offices.

The Lay Apostolate of Jesus Christ the Returning King

We seek to be united to Jesus in our daily work, and through our vocations, in order to obtain graces for the conversion of sinners. Through our cooperation with the Holy Spirit, we will allow Jesus to flow through us to the world, bringing His light. We do this in union with Mary, our Blessed Mother, with the Communion of Saints, with all of God's holy angels and with our fellow lay apostles in the world.

Guidelines for Lay Apostles

As lay apostles of Jesus Christ the Returning King, we agree to perform our basic obligations as practicing Catholics. Additionally, we will adopt the following spiritual practices, as best we can:

1. **Allegiance Prayer** and **Morning Offering**, plus a brief prayer for the Holy Father
2. **Eucharistic Adoration**, one hour per week
3. **Prayer Group Participation**, monthly, at which we pray the Luminous Mysteries of the Holy Rosary and read the Monthly Message
4. **Monthly Confession**
5. Further, we will follow the example of Jesus Christ as set out in the Holy Scripture, treating all others with His patience and kindness.

Allegiance Prayer

Dear God in Heaven, I pledge my allegiance to You. I give You my life, my work and my heart. In turn, give me the grace of obeying Your every direction to the fullest possible extent. Amen.

Morning Offering

O Jesus, through the Immaculate Heart of Mary, I offer You the prayers, works, joys and sufferings of this day, for all the intentions of Your Sacred Heart, in union with the Holy Sacrifice of the Mass throughout the world, in reparation for my sins, and for the intentions of the Holy Father. Amen.

Prayer for the Holy Father

Our Lady, Queen of the Church, protect our Holy Father, Francis, and bless his intentions.

Promise from Jesus to His Lay Apostles

May 12, 2005

Your message to souls remains constant. Welcome each soul to the rescue mission. You may assure each lay apostle that just as they concern themselves with My interests, I will concern Myself with theirs. They will be placed in My Sacred Heart and I will defend and protect them. I will also pursue complete conversion of each of their loved ones. So you see, the souls who serve in this rescue mission as My beloved lay apostles will know peace. The world cannot make this promise as only Heaven can bestow peace on a soul. This is truly Heaven's mission and I call every one of Heaven's children to assist Me. You will be well rewarded, My dear ones.

What about the Monthly Prayer Group?

Jesus asks us to form lay apostle prayer groups. He asks us to meet once each month to pray the Luminous Mysteries of the Holy Rosary and read the Monthly Message. A prayer group can be as small as two people within a family or as large as hundreds in a church.

Five Luminous Mysteries:

1. The Baptism of Jesus
2. The Wedding at Cana
3. The Proclamation of the Kingdom of God
4. The Transfiguration
5. The Institution of the Eucharist

Monthly Messages

For seven years Jesus gave Anne a message for the world on the first day of every month. Each month the apostolate reads and contemplates one of these monthly messages.

To receive the monthly messages you may access our website at **www.directionforourtimes.org** or call us at one of our offices to be placed on our mailing list.

We have also printed a book which contains all of the monthly messages. It can be purchased through our website as well.

Prayers taken from The Volumes

Prayers to God the Father

"What can I do for my Father in Heaven?"

"I trust You, God. I offer You my pain in the spirit of acceptance and I will serve You in every circumstance."

"God my Father in Heaven, You are all mercy. You love me and see my every sin. God, I call on You now as the Merciful Father. Forgive my every sin. Wash away the stains on my soul so that I may once again rest in complete innocence. I trust You, Father in Heaven. I rely on You. I thank You. Amen."

"God my Father, calm my spirit and direct my path."

"God, I have made mistakes. I am sorry. I am Your child, though, and seek to be united to You."

"I believe in God. I believe Jesus is calling me. I believe my Blessed Mother has requested my help. Therefore I am going to pray on this day and every day."

"God my Father, help me to understand."

Prayers to Jesus

"Jesus, I give You my day."

"Jesus, how do You want to use me on this day? You have a willing servant in me, Jesus. Allow me to work for the Kingdom."

"Lord, what can I do today to prepare for Your coming? Direct me, Lord, and I will see to Your wishes."

"Lord, help me."

"Jesus, love me."

Prayers to the Angels

"Angels from Heaven, direct my path."

"Dearest angel guardian, I desire to serve Jesus by remaining at peace. Please obtain for me the graces necessary to maintain His divine peace in my heart."

Prayers for a Struggling Soul

"Jesus, what do You think of all this? Jesus, what do You want me to do for this soul? Jesus, show me how to bring You into this situation."

"Angel guardian, thank you for your constant vigil over this soul. Saints in Heaven, please assist this dear angel."

Prayers for Children

"God in Heaven, You are the Creator of all things. Please send Your graces down upon our world."

"Jesus, I love You."

"Jesus, I trust in You. Jesus, I trust in You. Jesus, I trust in You."

"Jesus, I offer You my day."

"Mother Mary, help me to be good."

How to Pray the Rosary

1. Make the Sign of the Cross and say the "Apostles Creed."
2. Say the "Our Father."
3. Say three "Hail Marys."
4. Say the "Glory be to the Father."
5. Announce the First Mystery; then say the "Our Father."
6. Say ten "Hail Marys," while meditating on the Mystery.
7. Say the "Glory be to the Father." After each decade say the following prayer requested by the Blessed Virgin Mary at Fatima: "O my Jesus, forgive us our sins, save us from the fires of hell, lead all souls to Heaven, especially those in most need of Thy mercy."
8. Announce the Second Mystery: then say the "Our Father." Repeat 6 and 7 and continue with the Third, Fourth, and Fifth Mysteries in the same manner.
9. Say the "Hail, Holy Queen" on the medal after the five decades are completed.

As a general rule, depending on the season, the Joyful Mysteries are said on Monday and Saturday; the Sorrowful Mysteries on Tuesday and Friday;

the Glorious Mysteries on Wednesday and Sunday; and the Luminous Mysteries on Thursday.

Papal Reflections of the Mysteries

The Joyful Mysteries

The Joyful Mysteries are marked by the joy radiating from the event of the Incarnation. This is clear from the very first mystery, the Annunciation, where Gabriel's greeting to the Virgin of Nazareth is linked to an invitation to messianic joy: "Rejoice, Mary." The whole of salvation... had led up to this greeting. (Prayed on Mondays and Saturdays, and optional on Sundays during Advent and the Christmas Season.)

The Luminous Mysteries

Moving on from the infancy and the hidden life in Nazareth to the public life of Jesus, our contemplation brings us to those mysteries which may be called in a special way "Mysteries of Light." Certainly, the whole mystery of Christ is a mystery of light. He is the "Light of the world" (John 8:12). Yet this truth emerges in a special way during the years of His public life. (Prayed on Thursdays.)

The Sorrowful Mysteries

The Gospels give great prominence to the Sorrowful Mysteries of Christ. From the beginning, Christian piety, especially during the Lenten devotion of the Way of the Cross, has focused on the individual moments of the Passion, realizing that here is found the culmination of the revelation of God's love and the source of our salvation. (Prayed on Tuesdays and Fridays, and optional on Sundays during Lent.)

The Glorious Mysteries

"The contemplation of Christ's face cannot stop at the image of the Crucified One. He is the Risen One!" The Rosary has always expressed this knowledge born of faith and invited the believer to pass beyond the darkness of the Passion in order to gaze upon Christ's glory in the Resurrection and Ascension... Mary herself would be raised to that same glory in the Assumption. (Prayed on Wednesdays and Sundays.)

From the *Apostolic Letter The Rosary of the Virgin Mary*, Pope John Paul II, Oct. 16, 2002.

Prayers of the Rosary

The Sign of the Cross

In the name of the Father, and of the Son, and of the Holy Spirit. Amen.

The Apostles' Creed

I believe in God, the Father Almighty, Creator of Heaven and earth. I believe in Jesus Christ, His only Son, our Lord. He was conceived by the power of the Holy Spirit and born of the Virgin Mary. He suffered under Pontius Pilate, was crucified, died, and was buried. He descended into hell. On the third day He rose again from the dead. He ascended into Heaven, and is seated at the right hand of the Father. He will come again to judge the living and the dead. I believe in the Holy Spirit, the holy Catholic Church, the Communion of Saints, the forgiveness of sins, the resurrection of the body, and life everlasting. Amen.

Our Father

Our Father, who art in Heaven, hallowed be Thy name. Thy Kingdom come. Thy will be done on earth as it is in Heaven. Give us this day our daily bread. And forgive us our trespasses, as we forgive those who trespass against us. And lead us not into temptation, but deliver us from evil. Amen.

Hail Mary

Hail Mary, full of grace, the Lord is with thee. Blessed art thou among women, and blessed is the fruit of thy womb, Jesus. Holy Mary, Mother of God, pray for us sinners, now and at the hour of our death. Amen.

Glory Be to the Father

Glory be to the Father, and to the Son, and to the Holy Spirit. As it was in the beginning, is now, and ever shall be, world without end. Amen.

Hail Holy Queen

Hail, Holy Queen, Mother of Mercy, our life, our sweetness and our hope. To thee do we cry, poor banished children of Eve. To thee do we send up our sighs, mourning and weeping in this valley of tears. Turn then, most gracious Advocate, thine eyes of mercy towards us. And after this, our exile, show unto us the blessed fruit of thy womb, Jesus. O clement, O loving, O sweet Virgin Mary!

Pray for us, O Holy Mother of God.
That we may be made worthy of the promises of Christ.

The Mysteries

First Joyful Mystery:
The Annunciation

And when the angel had come to her, he said, "Hail, full of grace, the Lord is with thee. Blessed art thou among women." *(Luke* 1:28)

One *Our Father*, Ten *Hail Marys*,
One *Glory Be*, etc.

Fruit of the Mystery: ***Humility***

Second Joyful Mystery:
The Visitation

Elizabeth was filled with the Holy Spirit and cried out in a loud voice: "Blest are you among women and blest is the fruit of your womb."*(Luke* 1:41-42)

One *Our Father*, Ten *Hail Marys*,
One *Glory Be*, etc.

Fruit of the Mystery: ***Love of Neighbor***

Third Joyful Mystery:
The Birth of Jesus

She gave birth to her first-born Son and wrapped Him in swaddling clothes and laid Him in a manger, because there was no room for them in the place where travelers lodged. *(Luke* 2:7)

One *Our Father*, Ten *Hail Marys*,
One *Glory Be*, etc.

Fruit of the Mystery: ***Poverty***

Fourth Joyful Mystery:
The Presentation

When the day came to purify them according to the law of Moses, the couple brought Him up to Jerusalem so that He could be presented to the Lord, for it is written in the law of the Lord, "Every first-born male shall be consecrated to the Lord."

(Luke 2:22-23)

One *Our Father*, Ten *Hail Marys*,
One *Glory Be*, etc.

Fruit of the Mystery: ***Obedience***

Fifth Joyful Mystery:
The Finding of the Child Jesus in the Temple

On the third day they came upon Him in the temple sitting in the midst of the teachers, listening to them and asking them questions. *(Luke* 2:46)

One *Our Father*, Ten *Hail Marys*,
One *Glory Be*, etc.

Fruit of the Mystery: ***Joy in Finding Jesus***

First Luminous Mystery:
The Baptism of Jesus

And when Jesus was baptized... the heavens were opened and He saw the Spirit of God descending like a dove, and alighting on Him, and lo, a voice from heaven, saying "this is My beloved Son," with whom I am well pleased." *(Matthew* 3:16-17)

One *Our Father*, Ten *Hail Marys*,
One *Glory Be*, etc.

Fruit of the Mystery: ***Openness to the Holy Spirit***

Second Luminous Mystery:
The Wedding at Cana

His mother said to the servants, "Do whatever He tells you."… Jesus said to them, "Fill the jars with water." And they filled them up to the brim.

(John 2:5-7)

One *Our Father*, Ten *Hail Marys*,
One *Glory Be*, etc.

Fruit of the Mystery: ***To Jesus through Mary***

Third Luminous Mystery:
The Proclamation of the Kingdom of God

"And preach as you go, saying, 'The kingdom of heaven is at hand.' Heal the sick, raise the dead, cleanse lepers, cast out demons. You received without pay, give without pay." *(Matthew* 10:7-8)

One *Our Father*, Ten *Hail Marys*,
One *Glory Be*, etc.

Fruit of the Mystery: ***Repentance and Trust in God***

Fourth Luminous Mystery:
The Transfiguration

And as He was praying, the appearance of His countenance was altered and His raiment become dazzling white. And a voice came out of the cloud saying, "This is My Son, My chosen; listen to Him!

(Luke 9:29, 35)

One *Our Father*, Ten *Hail Marys*,
One *Glory Be*, etc.

Fruit of the Mystery: ***Desire for Holiness***

Fifth Luminous Mystery:
The Institution of the Eucharist

And He took bread, and when He had given thanks He broke it and gave it to them, saying, "This is My body which is given for you."... And likewise the cup after supper, saying, "This cup which is poured out for you is the new covenant in My blood."

(*Luke* 22:19-20)

One *Our Father*, Ten *Hail Marys*,
One *Glory Be*, etc.

Fruit of the Mystery: ***Adoration***

First Sorrowful Mystery:
The Agony in the Garden

In His anguish He prayed with all the greater intensity, and His sweat became like drops of blood falling to the ground. Then He rose from prayer and came to His disciples, only to find them asleep, exhausted with grief. (*Luke* 22:44-45)

One *Our Father*, Ten *Hail Marys*,
One *Glory Be*, etc.

Fruit of the Mystery: ***Sorrow for Sin***

Second Sorrowful Mystery:
The Scourging at the Pillar

Pilate's next move was to take Jesus and have Him scourged. (*John* 19:1)

One *Our Father*, Ten *Hail Marys*,
One *Glory Be*, etc.

Fruit of the Mystery: ***Purity***

Third Sorrowful Mystery:
The Crowning with Thorns

They stripped off His clothes and wrapped Him in a scarlet military cloak. Weaving a crown out of thorns they fixed it on His head, and stuck a reed in His right hand... *(Matthew 27:28-29)*

One *Our Father*, Ten *Hail Marys*,
One *Glory Be*, etc.

Fruit of the Mystery: ***Courage***

Fourth Sorrowful Mystery:
The Carrying of the Cross

... carrying the cross by Himself, He went out to what is called the Place of the Skull (in Hebrew, Golgotha). *(John 19:17)*

One *Our Father*, Ten *Hail Marys*,
One *Glory Be*, etc.

Fruit of the Mystery: ***Patience***

Fifth Sorrowful Mystery:
The Crucifixion

Jesus uttered a loud cry and said, "Father, into Your hands I commend My spirit." After He said this, He expired. *(Luke 23:46)*

One *Our Father*, Ten *Hail Marys*,
One *Glory Be*, etc.

Fruit of the Mystery: ***Perseverance***

First Glorious Mystery:
The Resurrection

You need not be amazed! You are looking for Jesus of Nazareth, the one who was crucified. He has been raised up; He is not here. See the place where they laid Him." *(Mark 16:6)*

One *Our Father*, Ten *Hail Marys*,
One *Glory Be*, etc.

Fruit of the Mystery: **Faith**

Second Glorious Mystery:
The Ascension

Then, after speaking to them, the Lord Jesus was taken up into Heaven and took His seat at God's right hand. *(Mark 16:19)*

One *Our Father*, Ten *Hail Marys*,
One *Glory Be*, etc.

Fruit of the Mystery: **Hope**

Third Glorious Mystery:
The Descent of the Holy Spirit

All were filled with the Holy Spirit. They began to express themselves in foreign tongues and make bold proclamation as the Spirit prompted them.
(Acts 2:4)

One *Our Father*, Ten *Hail Marys*,
One *Glory Be*, etc.

Fruit of the Mystery: **Love of God**

Fourth Glorious Mystery:
The Assumption

You are the glory of Jerusalem... you are the splendid boast of our people... God is pleased with what you have wrought. May you be blessed by the Lord Almighty forever and ever.

(Judith 15:9-10)

One *Our Father*, Ten *Hail Marys*,
One *Glory Be*, etc.

Fruit of the Mystery: ***Grace of a Happy Death***

Fifth Glorious Mystery:
The Coronation

A great sign appeared in the sky, a woman clothed with the sun, with the moon under her feet, and on her head a crown of twelve stars. *(Revelation* 12:1)

One *Our Father*, Ten *Hail Marys*,
One *Glory Be*, etc.

Fruit of the Mystery: ***Trust in Mary's Intercession***

How to Pray the Chaplet of Divine Mercy

The Chaplet of Divine Mercy is a prayer which Jesus taught St. Faustina Kowalska. The chaplet offers us a special means to pray for mercy for ourselves and the whole world.

The Chaplet of Mercy is recited using ordinary rosary beads of five decades. The chaplet is preceded by two opening prayers from the *Diary* of Saint Faustina and followed by a closing prayer.

1. Make the Sign of the Cross

2. Say the Two Opening Prayers

"You expired, Jesus, but the source of life gushed forth for souls, and the ocean of mercy opened up for the whole world. O Fount of Life, unfathomable Divine Mercy, envelop the whole world and empty Yourself out upon us."

"O Blood and Water, which gushed forth from the Heart of Jesus as a fountain of mercy for us, I trust in You!"

3. Say the Our Father

4. Say the Hail Mary

5. Say the Apostles' Creed

6. On each large bead pray the Eternal Father Prayer:

"Eternal Father, I offer You the Body and Blood, Soul and Divinity of Your dearly beloved Son, our Lord, Jesus Christ, in atonement for our sins and those of the whole world."

7. On each of the ten small beads of the decade pray:

"For the sake of His Sorrowful Passion, have mercy on us and on the whole world."

8. Repeat prayers 6 and 7 for the remaining decades

Concluding Prayers

9. Say the Holy God prayer three times

"Holy God, Holy Mighty One, Holy Immortal One, have mercy on us and on the whole world."

10. Optional Closing Prayer

"Eternal God, in whom mercy is endless and the treasury of compassion inexhaustible, look kindly upon us and increase Your mercy in us, that in difficult moments we might not despair nor become despondent, but with great confidence submit ourselves to Your holy will, which is Love and Mercy itself."

To learn more about the image of The Divine Mercy, the Chaplet of Divine Mercy and the series of revelations given to St. Faustina Kowalska please contact:

Marians of the Immaculate Conception
Stockbridge, Massachusetts 01263
Telephone 800-462-7426
www.marian.org

The Volumes

Direction for Our Times
as given to Anne, a lay apostle

Volume One: *Thoughts on Spirituality*

Volume Two: *Conversations with the*
                       Eucharistic Heart of Jesus

Volume Three: *God the Father Speaks to*
                       His Children
                       The Blessed Mother Speaks to
                       Her Bishops and Priests

Volume Four: *Jesus the King*
                       Heaven Speaks to Priests
                       Jesus Speaks to Sinners

Volume Five: *Jesus the Redeemer*

Volume Six: *Heaven Speaks to Families*

Volume Seven: *Greetings from Heaven*

Volume Eight: *Resting in the Heart of the Savior*

Volume Nine: *Angels*

Volume Ten: *Jesus Speaks to His Apostles*

The Volumes are now available in PDF format for
free download and printing from our website:
www.directionforourtimes.org.
We encourage everyone to print and distribute them.

The Volumes are also available at your local bookstore.

The "Heaven Speaks" Booklets

Direction for Our Times
as given to Anne, a lay apostle

The following booklets are available individually from Direction for Our Times:

Heaven Speaks About Abortion
Heaven Speaks About Addictions
Heaven Speaks to Victims of Clerical Abuse
Heaven Speaks to Consecrated Souls
Heaven Speaks About Depression
Heaven Speaks About Divorce
Heaven Speaks to Prisoners
Heaven Speaks to Soldiers
Heaven Speaks About Stress
Heaven Speaks to Young Adults

Heaven Speaks to Those Away from the Church
Heaven Speaks to Those Considering Suicide
Heaven Speaks to Those Who Do Not Know Jesus
Heaven Speaks to Those Who Are Dying
Heaven Speaks to Those Who Experience Tragedy
Heaven Speaks to Those Who Fear Purgatory
Heaven Speaks to Those Who Have Rejected God
Heaven Speaks to Those Who Struggle to Forgive
Heaven Speaks to Those Who Suffer from Financial Need
Heaven Speaks to Parents Who Worry About Their Children's Salvation

All twenty of the "Heaven Speaks" booklets are now available in PDF format for free download and printing from our website www.directionforourtimes.org. We encourage everyone to print and distribute these booklets.

Other books by Anne, a lay apostle

Climbing the Mountain
Discovering your path to holiness
Anne's experiences of Heaven

The Mist of Mercy
Spiritual Warfare
Anne's experiences of Purgatory

Serving In Clarity
A Guide for Lay Apostles
of Jesus Christ the Returning King

In Defense of Obedience
and
Reflections on the Priesthood
Two Essays on topics close to the Heart of Jesus

Lessons in Love
Moving Toward Divine Intimacy

Whispers from the Cross
Reclaiming the Church
Through Personal Holiness

Transforming Grace
Becoming Thoughtful Men and Women of God

Purgatory, Prayer and Forgiveness